Journeys Of Professor X

by

Ryan R. Pecson

COPYRIGHT 2023 TIME'S QUEST

By Ryan R. Pecson

ISBN

Hardbound-978-621-470-845-1

MOBI/KINDLE-978-621-470-846-8

Softbound/Paperback-978-621-470-847-5

Published by:

Poetry Planet Book Publishing House

Rosario, Pozorrubio, Pangasinan, Philippines

Contact Number: 09554960094

Email: maritesritumalta@gmail.com

To my daughter, Tiara Jane:

You are the best gift that I received from the Lord.

To my parents, Mario and Erlinda:

You are my life's inspiration.

*To my siblings, Marlene (†), Dyan, Lucia, Marlon,
and Leslie Ann:*

You are my cornerstones.

*To my nephews, Kiba and Zayne; and my nieces,
Yumi, Hana, and Sydney:*

You are my happy pill.

"Once there was a man who was afraid of his
shadow. Then he met it.

Now he glows in the dark."

Ben Loory

CONTENTS

AUTHOR'S NOTE

Here are the adventures of Professor X into the
realms of life's paradoxes. I hope you like
them.

- R.R.P.

Chapter 1

UNWAVERING HOPE: RESILIENCE UNVEILED

***

"To live is the rarest thing in the world. Most people exist, that is all."

Oscar Wilde

***

In a bustling classroom, I stood before a group of eager students, ready to impart a lesson that would shape their perspectives on resilience and optimism. Today's topic was the intriguing Stockdale Paradox—a concept that defied conventional thinking and captivated minds with its profound implications.

With a warm greeting, I set the stage for our journey into the depths of the Stockdale Paradox. The students leaned forward, curiosity sparked, as I promised to share a story that embodied the very essence of this paradox.

I began to recount the incredible tale of James Stockdale, a true hero amidst the horrors of the Vietnam War. As a prisoner of war, Stockdale endured unimaginable suffering and grappled with the uncertainty of captivity. Yet, amid darkness, he displayed a remarkable sense of resilience that would become legendary.

"As a POW, Stockdale faced brutal conditions and relentless challenges," I continued, vividly painting his struggle. "But what set him apart was his unwavering hope—a belief that he would ultimately triumph, despite the harsh realities he confronted."

A hushed silence enveloped the classroom as the significance of Stockdale's mindset settled upon the students' minds. Their eyes sparkled with curiosity and admiration for this indomitable spirit.

"We can learn a valuable lesson from Stockdale," I emphasized, my voice filled with conviction. "It's not about denying the difficulties we face; rather, it's the ability to confront those challenges head-on while maintaining an unwavering hope for a better future."

A student's hand shot up, eager to delve deeper into this paradox. "But, Professor X, isn't there a contradiction between being realistic about our circumstances and staying optimistic?"

I smiled, impressed by their thoughtful engagement. "Ah, you've touched upon a crucial point," I replied. "The key is to strike a balance—a delicate harmony between accepting the present reality and believing in our capacity to shape our own destiny. Embracing the challenges with a realistic mindset empowers us to develop strategies to overcome them, while unwavering hope fuels our determination to prevail."

As the class concluded, the students left with a new found understanding of the Stockdale Paradox. They were inspired by Stockdale's indomitable spirit and eager to apply the principles of resilience and unwavering hope in their own lives.

As I watched them depart, I couldn't help but feel a sense of pride. The Stockdale Paradox had captivated their minds and hearts, and I knew it would remain etched in their souls, propelling them forward with strength and determination to navigate life's obstacles. The journey into the depths of resilience had just begun, and I was eager to witness the transformative impact of the Stockdale Paradox on their lives.

***

Questions to Ponder

1. How can we apply the Stockdale Paradox in our own lives when faced with challenging situations or setbacks?

2. In what ways can accepting harsh realities while maintaining hope and optimism lead to personal growth and resilience?

3. Reflecting on the story of James Stockdale, what qualities or mindset allowed him to endure years of captivity and emerge as a hero?

4. How can we balance realism and optimism daily, especially when confronted with adversity?

5. Consider the impact of the Stockdale Paradox on decision-making. How might embracing the paradox influence our

choices and approach to achieving our goals?

INTO THE DEPTHS

***

"Your perception of my exterior may not match what lies beneath the surface."

Kamil Ali

***

In a serene classroom, I stood before a group of curious students, eager to unravel the mysteries of The Iceberg Paradox. This enchanting concept would challenge their perceptions of identity and human complexity.

With a warm smile, I greeted my attentive audience. "Good morning, class! Today, we embark on a journey into the depths of The Iceberg Paradox—an idea that reveals the hidden layers beneath the surface of every individual."

The students leaned forward, their curiosity piqued by the allure of the enigmatic paradox. I began to share a story that would illustrate the profound implications of The Iceberg Paradox in a captivating manner.

"Imagine," I continued, "a majestic iceberg adrift in the vast ocean. What we see above the waterline is merely a fraction of its grandeur. Beneath the surface lies an intricate and vast structure, concealing immense depth and complexity."

A hush fell over the room as the students visualized the metaphorical iceberg. Their imaginations took flight, contemplating the deeper layers hidden from the naked eye.

"In our everyday lives, we encounter others and often judge them based on what meets the eye," I explained. "But beneath that facade lies a symphony of emotions, experiences, dreams, and fears that form the core of their true identity. The Iceberg Paradox beckons us to peer beyond the obvious and seek a deeper understanding of one another."

Brimming with curiosity, a student raised a hand to ask a question. "Professor X, how can we navigate this paradox in our interactions with others? How can we truly explore the depths that lie beneath?"

I welcomed their inquiry with a warm smile, appreciating their engagement. "It begins with curiosity and empathy," I replied. "Engage in meaningful conversations, listen with intent, and be open to discovering the myriad layers that make each person unique. Embrace the complexities of others, and approach them with a compassionate heart."

As the class concluded, the students left with a new found perspective on The Iceberg Paradox. They carried with them the understanding that human beings are multi-dimensional, each one an intricate tapestry of experiences and emotions. Inspired to delve into their identities, they set forth into the world with curiosity and understanding.

I watched them depart, hopeful that this lesson would transform their interactions, fostering deeper connections and an appreciation for the nuanced beauty within every individual. The Iceberg Paradox would forever serve as a guiding beacon, reminding them to see beyond the surface and embrace the enchanting complexities that make each person an awe-inspiring wonder.

Questions to Ponder

1. How does The Iceberg Paradox challenge our tendency to judge others based solely on surface-level observations?

2. Reflecting on the metaphor of the iceberg, what implications does it have for our understanding of self and the layers of our identities that may be hidden beneath the surface?

3. In what ways can curiosity and empathy foster a deeper understanding of others and help us navigate The Iceberg Paradox in our interactions?

4. Consider the impact of embracing the complexities of others on our ability to form meaningful connections and relationships. How might our perceptions and interactions change when we recognize the depth beneath the surface?

5. How can the awareness of The Iceberg Paradox influence our approach to diversity and inclusion, encouraging us to value and respect the uniqueness and hidden stories of individuals?

Chapter 3

REALM OF IMAGINATION

***

"Imagination is the beginning of creation. You imagine what you desire, you will what you imagine, and at last, you create what

you will."

George Bernard Shaw

***

In a world where the boundaries of science and imagination intertwined, I stood before my eager students, ready to ignite their minds with the captivating concept of the Region Beta Paradox. This paradox would challenge their perception of reality and the profound power of their thoughts.

With enthusiasm, I greeted the class, "Good morning, everyone! Today, we embark on a thrilling journey into the enigmatic realm of the Region Beta Paradox. It delves into the mesmerizing connection between our thoughts and the tangible manifestation of our world."

The students leaned forward, their eyes alight with anticipation. I knew this lesson would spark their imaginations and provoke deep contemplation. As I began to share a remarkable story, the classroom brimmed with curiosity.

"In the mysterious Region Beta, the inhabitants possess an extraordinary ability — to bring their thoughts to life," I narrated. "Imagine conjuring your wildest dreams into reality simply by envisioning them."

A sense of wonder permeated the room as the students immersed themselves in infinite possibilities. They yearned to explore a world where imagination danced hand-in-hand with reality.

"But here's the twist," I continued, a mischievous glint in my eye. "In the Region Beta Paradox, thoughts not only shape the world of one's desires but also unveil their deepest fears and insecurities."

A collective gasp echoed as the students absorbed the paradox's profound revelation.

The power to create their reality came with the responsibility of confronting their innermost demons.

"The key to mastering the Region Beta lies in self-awareness," I elucidated. "By acknowledging and embracing their fears, individuals can harness their thoughts as catalysts for personal growth."

Eager hands shot up, and the class became a vibrant discussion forum. The students delved deeper into the paradox, exploring the nature of their own thoughts and the potential to wield them as instruments of transformation.

As the class drew close, the students departed with a newfound understanding of the Region Beta Paradox. They carried with them the realization that their thoughts held immense power—the power to shape their world and confront their fears and evolve.

I watched them leave, confident that this lesson would inspire them to embrace self-reflection and consciously direct their thoughts toward creating a reality infused with joy, growth, and authenticity. The Region Beta Paradox had unlocked the gates to the boundless realm of their consciousness, urging them to embrace their inner strengths and transform their perceived limitations. The journey into Region Beta had just begun in a world where the imaginable and the tangible intertwined.

***

Questions to Ponder

1. How does the Region Beta Paradox concept challenge our understanding of the relationship between thoughts and reality?

2. In what ways can self-awareness and mindfulness of our thoughts help us navigate the Region Beta Paradox?

3. Reflecting on the story, what lessons can we draw about the potential consequences of our thoughts and the importance of addressing our fears and insecurities?

4. How might the Region Beta Paradox influence our perceptions of personal responsibility and accountability for the reality we experience?

5. Considering the power of thoughts in shaping our reality, what strategies can we

employ to consciously direct our thoughts toward creating a positive and fulfilling existence?

Chapter 4

THE GREAT BALANCING ACT

***

"Be moderate in order to taste the joys of life in abundance."

Epicurus

***

In the quiet classroom, I stood before my students, ready to delve into the enigmatic concept of The Paradox of Self-Awareness. It was a profound exploration of the human psyche, the delicate balance between knowing oneself and the potential dangers that lie within.

"Good day, class!" I greeted them with a contemplative expression. "Today, we embark on a journey into the depths of The Paradox of Self-Awareness. It is the notion that while self-awareness can lead to personal growth and understanding, it can also uncover uncomfortable truths and ignite inner conflicts."

The students leaned in, their eyes filled with curiosity. I began weaving a tale that would challenge their perceptions.

"Imagine," I continued, "gaining deep insight into your own thoughts, emotions, and motivations. It is a gift, but it also comes with the burden of self-examination. The more we understand ourselves, the more we confront our flaws, vulnerabilities, and the shadows that lurk within."

A silence enveloped the room as the students absorbed the weight of this paradox. The power of self-awareness intrigued them, but its potential for discomfort lingered.

"To navigate The Paradox of Self-Awareness," I explained, "we must cultivate self-compassion. Acknowledge your imperfections, but also embrace the beauty of your strengths. It is the delicate dance of self-discovery and self-acceptance."

One student raised their hand, their voice filled with uncertainty. "Professor X, how can we balance self-awareness and self-criticism? Isn't it a thin line?"

I smiled, appreciating their thoughtful question. "Indeed, it is a delicate balance. Self-awareness allows us to recognize areas for growth without falling into the trap of self-condemnation. Treat yourself with kindness and nurture a growth mindset."

As the class drew close, the students departed with a newfound understanding of The Paradox of Self-Awareness. They carried with them the realization that self-discovery requires both courage and compassion. They were inspired to embark on the journey of self-awareness, embracing their strengths and addressing their weaknesses without losing sight of their inherent worth.

I watched them leave, hopeful that this lesson would guide them toward a profound understanding of themselves and foster a foundation of self-compassion. The Paradox of Self-Awareness would forever remind them that they could find the keys to personal growth and fulfillment within the depths of their complexities.

Questions to Ponder

1. How can self-awareness lead to personal growth and understanding, and what potential challenges or conflicts might arise from delving deep into our own psyche?

2. Reflecting on self-compassion, how can we balance acknowledging our flaws and nurturing a positive self-image?

3. In what ways can the Paradox of Self-Awareness impact our relationships with others? How does self-awareness influence our interactions and perceptions of those around us?

4. Consider the significance of self-acceptance in navigating the Paradox of Self-Awareness. How can embracing both our strengths and vulnerabilities contribute to our overall well-being?

5. How might exploring self-awareness and self-compassion influence our ability to make meaningful choices and live more authentically and fulfilled lives?

Chapter 5

CHANGE AND CALCULATED RISKS

***

"To become a better you, dare to take
calculated risks and overcome your limitations.
Your scars can make

you a star, but you have

to decide."

Israelmore Ayivor

***

In the bustling classroom, I stood before my students, ready to delve into the intriguing concept of the Stability-Instability Paradox. It was a subject that would challenge their perceptions of equilibrium, change, and the delicate interplay between the two.

"Hello, class!" I greeted them with enthusiasm. "Today, we embark on a journey into the captivating realm of the Stability-Instability

Paradox. It suggests that stability can breed complacency while embracing a certain level of instability can foster growth and progress."

The students leaned forward, their interest piqued by the paradoxical nature of the topic. I began to share a story that would illustrate the paradox and ignite their contemplation.

"Imagine," I continued, "a tree rooted deeply in the ground, standing tall and stable. It appears unyielding. However, if it never sways in the wind, its roots remain shallow, and it lacks the resilience needed to withstand storms."

Silence fell over the room as the students visualized the steadfast tree and contemplated the implications of this concept in their own lives.

"The Stability-Instability Paradox teaches us that there is inherent strength in embracing change and taking calculated risks," I explained. "By stepping outside our comfort zones and venturing into the realm of uncertainty, we open ourselves to new opportunities, personal growth, and resilience."

A student raised their hand, curiosity evident in their eyes. "Professor X, how can we find the balance between stability and instability in our own lives? How can we embrace change without feeling overwhelmed or losing our sense of grounding?"

I smiled, appreciating their thoughtful question. "It begins with self-awareness and a willingness to push beyond our perceived limits," I replied. "We must assess our current state of stability and identify areas where growth and change are needed. By embracing calculated risks, learning from setbacks, and adapting to new circumstances, we can find a dynamic equilibrium that allows for stability within the context of progress."

As the class drew close, the students left with a newfound perspective on the Stability-Instability Paradox. They carried with them the understanding that while stability offers comfort, it is through embracing a certain level of instability that we can truly thrive and evolve. They were inspired to embrace change, take calculated risks, and foster a balance that nurtured stability and growth.

I watched them depart, hopeful that this lesson would remind them to seek a dynamic equilibrium in their lives, embracing the inherent paradoxes that propel them forward. The Stability-Instability Paradox will forever guide them toward personal growth and resilience.

***

Questions to Ponder

1. How does the Stability-Instability Paradox challenge our conventional understanding of stability as a fixed and unchanging state and encourage us to embrace change and calculated risks for personal growth?

2. Reflecting on the tree metaphor, what can we learn about the importance of flexibility and resilience in navigating life's challenges? How can we strike a balance between stability and the need for growth?

3. How can we identify areas in our lives where stability may have led to complacency, and how can we introduce a healthy level of instability to foster personal and professional development?

4. Consider the role of self-awareness in finding the balance between stability and instability. How can we cultivate a mindset that is open to change and willing to step outside our comfort zones while still maintaining a sense of grounding?

5. How might understanding the Stability-Instability Paradox influence our decision-making process and approach to risks? How can we make informed choices that foster growth and progress while maintaining stability and security?

Chapter 6

HIT WITH PRECISION

***

"A goal without a plan is only a dream."

Brian Tracy

***

In the tranquil setting of the archery range, I stood before my students, ready to unravel the mysteries of the Archer's Paradox. It was a concept that would challenge their understanding of precision, technique, and the delicate interplay between physics and skill.

"Welcome, class!" I greeted them with a smile. "Today, we embark on an exploration of the Archer's Paradox. The enigmatic phenomenon occurs when an arrow flexes and bends as it is released from the bow, yet somehow manages to hit the intended target."

The students leaned forward; their eyes filled with curiosity. I began to share a story that would illustrate the paradox and ignite their fascination.

"Imagine," I continued, "an archer drawing back their bowstring with focused determination. The arrow's trajectory seems uncertain, defying the logic of a straight path. And yet, miraculously, it finds its mark."

A sense of wonder filled the air as the students visualized the archer's skill and the paradoxical nature of the arrow's flight. They pondered the implications of this concept on their own pursuits of mastery.

"The Archer's Paradox teaches us that precision is not always achieved through rigidity," I explained. "Sometimes, flexibility and adaptation are necessary. The archer must understand the physics at play, honing their technique to harness the paradox and accurately deliver the arrow."

A student raised their hand, their voice filled with curiosity. "Professor X, how can we apply the lessons of the Archer's Paradox to our own lives and endeavors? How can we embrace flexibility while still striving for precision?"

I smiled, appreciating their thoughtful question. "It begins with a deep understanding of our craft," I replied. "We must study and practice, developing a foundation of knowledge and skill. But we must also remain open to adaptability, willing to adjust our approach as circumstances change. Embrace the paradox of balance between rigidity and flexibility, and find the harmony that allows for precise execution."

As the class drew close, the students left with a newfound perspective on the Archer's Paradox. They carried with them the understanding that sometimes, achieving mastery requires embracing the inherent complexities and contradictions. They were inspired to approach their pursuits with precision and adaptability, seeking to find the delicate balance that allows growth and success.

I watched them depart, hopeful that this lesson would remind them of the intricate interplay between skill, flexibility, and precision in all aspects of life. The Archer's Paradox would remind them that the path to excellence lies within the paradox.

***

Questions to Ponder

1. How does Archer's Paradox challenge our perception of precision and mastery, highlighting the role of flexibility and adaptation in achieving accuracy?

2. Reflecting on the archer's arrow metaphor, what can we learn about the delicate balance between structure and fluidity in our own pursuits of excellence?

3. How can we apply the lessons of the Archer's Paradox to our lives and endeavors, embracing adaptability while striving for precision?

4. Consider the significance of understanding the underlying physics and principles of a craft. How can this knowledge enhance our ability to harness the paradoxes within our chosen fields and achieve mastery?

5. How might Archer's Paradox influence our approach to challenges and setbacks? How can we use flexibility and adaptability to navigate obstacles and adjust our strategies to hit our targets?

Chapter 7

TIME TO MAKE A CHOICE

***

"Nothing is more difficult, and therefore more precious, than to be able to decide."

Napoleon Bonaparte

***

As the classroom buzzed with anticipation, I was eager to impart knowledge. As a young teacher, I introduced my students to the paradox of choice.

"Good morning, class!" I greeted them with a smile. "Today, we delve into the fascinating paradox of choice. It suggests that while options can empower us, they can lead to indecision and dissatisfaction. To understand this concept, we'll embark on a hands-on activity."

The students leaned forward, intrigued by the challenge that awaited them. I distributed various colorful candies to each student and explained the task.

"Your mission is to select one candy from the assortment provided. But here's the catch—you cannot change it once you choose. Think carefully, for you will experience the paradox of choice firsthand."

The room grew quiet as the students contemplated their options. Some were drawn to the vibrant gummies, while others eyed the chocolate bars. The variety overwhelmed them.

After several moments of deliberation, the students made their selections. Their faces displayed a mix of satisfaction and curiosity, knowing they had made their choices but pondering what they had foregone.

We gathered in a circle, and I encouraged them to share their experiences. They spoke of the excitement of choosing and the pang of regret over what they hadn't selected. We discussed the notion of satisfaction and how having fewer options might lead to a more profound sense of contentment.

As the bell rang, signaling the end of the class, the students left with a newfound understanding of the paradox of choice. They realized that while options can be liberating, they must also be approached with mindfulness and an awareness of the trade-offs involved.

I watched them depart, hopeful that this lesson would serve as a guiding light in their future decision-making. The paradox of choice would forever be imprinted in their minds, reminding them to seek balance and purpose in a world filled with limitless possibilities.

***

Questions to Ponder

1. How does the paradox of choice challenge our traditional notions of freedom and empowerment?

2. How can the experience of the hands-on activity with the candies help us grasp the inherent trade-offs and limitations of choice?

3. Reflecting on the students' discussions about satisfaction and regret, what insights can we gain about the emotional impact of making choices and the potential for dissatisfaction?

4. How might a greater awareness of the paradox of choice influence our decision-making processes and lead to more mindful and intentional choices?

5. Considering the lasting impact of this lesson on the students, what strategies can we employ to navigate the abundance of choices we encounter in our daily lives while fostering a sense of contentment and fulfillment?

Chapter 8

TO THE TOP

***

"Don't limit yourself. Many people limit themselves to what they think they

can do. You can go as far as your

mind lets you. What you

believe, you can

achieve."

Mary Kay Ash

***

In the vibrant classroom, I stood before my students, ready to unravel the mysteries of The Ladder Paradox. It was a concept that would challenge their perceptions of progress and success, urging them to reflect on their personal journeys.

"Good day, class!" I greeted them with a smile. "Today, we embark on a thought-provoking exploration of The Ladder Paradox. It invites us to reconsider the conventional notion of climbing the ladder of success."

The students leaned in; their eyes filled with curiosity. I began to share a story that would illustrate the paradox and ignite their contemplation.

"Imagine," I continued, "a ladder stretching endlessly towards the sky. Each rung represents a milestone of achievement, whether academic, professional, or personal. We are often told to strive for the top, believing it to be the pinnacle of success."

A hush fell over the room as the students envisioned the ladder and its infinite ascent. They pondered the implications of this paradox on their own lives and aspirations.

"The Ladder Paradox challenges us to question whether the pursuit of vertical progress truly leads to fulfillment," I explained. "What if success is not solely defined by reaching the top but by the growth and experiences we encounter?"

A student raised their hand, a spark of curiosity in their eyes. "Professor X, how can we reconcile our desire for achievement with the idea of The Ladder Paradox? How can we find balance?"

I smiled, appreciating their thoughtfulness. "It begins with embracing the journey itself," I replied. "Acknowledge that progress comes in various forms, not just reaching the highest rung. Cultivate gratitude for each step and focus on personal growth rather than comparing your position to others."

As the class concluded, the students left with a new found perspective on The Ladder Paradox. They understood that success is not solely determined by vertical ascent but by the meaningful experiences, lessons, and connections made along the way. They were inspired to redefine their own measures of success and find joy in pursuing growth.

I watched them depart, hopeful that this lesson would empower them to embrace their unique paths and celebrate the beauty of their personal journeys. The Ladder Paradox would forever serve as a reminder to appreciate the process rather than being solely fixated on the destination.

***

Questions to Ponder

1. How does The Ladder Paradox challenge our conventional notions of success and achievement, encouraging us to reevaluate the meaning of progress?

2. Reflecting on the ladder metaphor, what does it reveal about the importance of personal growth, experiences, and connections along our journey rather than solely focusing on reaching the top?

3. How can we balance striving for personal goals and finding contentment in the present moment, embracing the process rather than being fixated on the result?

4. Consider the impact of comparing ourselves to others on our perception of success. How can we shift our mindset to appreciate our own unique journeys, free from the pressure of societal expectations?

5. How might embracing The Ladder Paradox influence our goal-setting and pursuit fulfillment? How can we redefine our measures of success to align with our personal values and aspirations rather than society's predefined notions?

Chapter 9

HIDDEN WONDERS

***

"We carry within us the wonders we seek
without us."

Thomas Browne

***

In the dimly lit classroom, I prepared to captivate his students with the enigmatic concept of the Dark Sky Paradox. It was a topic that would challenge their perception of darkness, light, and the hidden wonders within.

"Greetings, class!" I exclaimed, his eyes shimmering with intrigue. "Today, we embark on a journey into the mesmerizing realm of the Dark Sky Paradox. It suggests we can discover the most magnificent celestial wonders in darkness."

The students leaned forward; their curiosity ignited by the paradoxical nature of the subject.

I began to weave a story that would unravel the mysteries of the night sky.

"Imagine," I continued, "a moonless night shrouded in darkness. To the ordinary eye, it may seem void of beauty and life. But if you gaze up at the heavens with patience and wonder, you will witness the constellations, shooting stars, and the ethereal glow of distant galaxies."

Silence enveloped the room as the students imagined the vast expanse of the night sky and contemplated the hidden treasures concealed within.

"The Dark Sky Paradox teaches us that sometimes, it is in the absence of light that the true brilliance of the universe reveals itself," I explained. "It encourages us to embrace the darkness, to seek solace in the unknown, and to find beauty in what may initially seem void."

A student raised their hand, their voice filled with curiosity. "Professor X, how can we apply the lessons of the Dark Sky Paradox to our own lives? How can we find beauty and inspiration in times of darkness and uncertainty?"

I smiled, appreciating their thoughtful question. "It begins with cultivating a sense of curiosity and open-mindedness," I replied. "In the face of challenges and moments of darkness, we can see them as opportunities for growth, transformation, and self-discovery. By embracing the unknown, we allow ourselves to uncover hidden strengths and find beauty in the most unexpected places."

As the class drew close, the students left with a new found perspective on the Dark Sky Paradox. They carried with them the understanding that darkness can hold its own enchantment and that in the depths of uncertainty, there is room for growth and revelation. They were inspired to seek beauty in all aspects of life, even in the moments that may appear devoid of light.

I watched them depart, hopeful that this lesson would serve as a guiding light in their journey. The Dark Sky Paradox would forever remind them to look beyond the surface, embrace the unknown, and discover the hidden wonders that await in the depths of darkness.

***

Questions to Ponder

1. How does the Dark Sky Paradox challenge our perception of darkness as a negative or empty space and encourage us to find beauty and inspiration in moments of uncertainty and the unknown?

2. Reflecting on the metaphor of the night sky, what can we learn about the importance of patience, curiosity, and open-mindedness in discovering hidden treasures and possibilities in life?

3. How can we apply the lessons of the Dark Sky Paradox to navigate through challenging times, finding resilience and strength in moments of darkness?

4. Consider the role of perspective and mindset in embracing the unknown and finding beauty in unexpected places. How can we cultivate an attitude that sees opportunities for growth and transformation even in the face of uncertainty?

5. How might the understanding of the Dark Sky Paradox influence our appreciation for

the beauty and wonder of the universe?
How can we carry this perspective into our
daily lives, finding moments of awe and
inspiration in the ordinary and
extraordinary?

Chapter 10

INTRICACY OF CONNECTEDNESS

***

"Invisible threads are the strongest ties."

Friedrich Nietzsche

***

In the bustling classroom, I stood before his students, ready to unravel the enigmatic concept of the Bootstrap Paradox. It was a subject that would challenge their understanding of causality, time loops, and the intricate web of interconnected events.

"Welcome, class!" I greeted them with a twinkle in my eyes. "Today, we venture into the captivating realm of the Bootstrap Paradox. It suggests that an object or information can exist without origin, caught in an endless causality loop."

The students leaned forward; their curiosity piqued by the mind-bending nature of the topic.

I began to share a story that would illustrate the paradox and ignite their contemplation.

"Imagine," I continued, "a traveler who journeys back in time and delivers a groundbreaking invention to a brilliant scientist. The scientist, inspired by this gift, uses the invention to create it, unknowingly becoming the source of its existence. The question arises: where did the invention truly originate?"

Silence filled the room as the students grappled with the complexities of the paradox and contemplated the nature of cause and effect.

"The Bootstrap Paradox challenges our understanding of linear time and the notion of originality," I explained. "It asks us to consider the possibility that information or objects can exist without a clear origin, caught in an eternal loop of creation and discovery."

A student raised their hand; their voice tinged with fascination. "Professor X, how can we make sense of the Bootstrap Paradox? Does it imply that there is no true beginning or end?

I smiled, appreciating their thoughtful question. "The Bootstrap Paradox invites us to question our assumptions about causality and the linear progression of time," he replied. "While it may challenge our traditional understanding, it also encourages us to embrace the complexity and interconnection of events. It reminds us that every action, every invention, and every discovery is intertwined with the fabric of time itself."

The students left with a renewed perspective on the Bootstrap Paradox as the class drew close. They carried with them the understanding that the nature of time is a tapestry woven with intricate loops, where the past, present, and future are entangled in a continuum. They were inspired to explore the mysteries of causality and ponder the possibilities of the unbreakable cycles within the universe.

I watched them depart, hopeful that this lesson would catalyze their further exploration of the enigmatic paradoxes in the fabric of time. The Bootstrap Paradox would forever ignite their curiosity, urging them to question the boundaries of existence and the intricate dance of cause and effect.

***

Questions to Ponder

1. How does the Bootstrap Paradox challenge our traditional understanding of causality and the linear progression of time? How does it invite us to question the notion of originality and a clear origin?

2. Reflecting on the story presented, what implications does the Bootstrap Paradox have for understanding free will and determinism? Does the existence of information or objects without a clear origin suggest a predetermined fate or a more complex interplay of choices and consequences?

3. In what ways does the Bootstrap Paradox highlight the interconnections of events and the intricate loops within the fabric of time? How can this perspective shape our understanding of the past, present, and future as a continuum rather than distinct moments?

4. Consider the ethical implications of the Bootstrap Paradox. If an invention or knowledge exists in an eternal loop with no clear original creator, how does this impact

our attribution of credit and intellectual property?

5. How can exploring the Bootstrap Paradox influence our perception of personal identity and the narratives we construct about ourselves? Does the paradox challenge the notion of a singular, linear identity or offer new insights into the complex layers of our existence?

Chapter 11

ANTICIPATING DESIRES

***

"Expecting is the greatest impediment to living. In anticipation of tomorrow,

it loses today."

Lucius Annaeus Seneca

***

In the vibrant and electric atmosphere of the bustling classroom, I stood at the front, eager to ignite the minds of my students with a tale of intellectual intrigue—the enigmatic Bartender Paradox. As they settled into their seats, their eyes sparked with curiosity, hungry for the mental feast ahead.

"Hello, my dear students!" I greeted them with a warm smile, my excitement palpable. "Today, we embark on a journey into the fascinating world of the Bartender Paradox—a paradox that unfurls the intricate dance between bartenders and their customers."

The class leaned in, spellbound by the prospect of unraveling this tantalizing enigma. I continued, "Picture a bartender whose skills transcend the ordinary—they possess an uncanny ability to fathom the deepest desires of their patrons. With finesse and intuition, they craft the perfect drink for each person, even before a single word is spoken as if they can read their souls."

The students exchanged intrigued glances, their imaginations running wild with the possibilities such a bartender could bring to life. Raising an eyebrow, I posed the question at the heart of the paradox, "But here lies the conundrum: if the bartender knows the exact drink a customer desires before they even voice it, does the customer genuinely possess free will in their choice?"

A hush fell over the room as the students grappled with the complexities of the paradox, the wheels of their minds spinning furiously. I continued, "The Bartender Paradox shakes the foundation of our belief in free will, suggesting that our choices might already be foreseen and influenced by forces beyond our control."

Eager to explore this philosophical labyrinth, a student's hand shot up, and their voice brimming with curiosity, they asked, "Professor X, how do we reconcile this paradox with our yearning for autonomy and the conviction that our decisions are our own?"

A knowing smile spread across my face, relishing the opportunity to engage them in the heart of the paradox. "Ah, my astute student," I replied, "the Bartender Paradox beckons us to venture into determinism and free will. While it challenges the notion of absolute autonomy, it also reminds us of the intricate web connecting our choices with the tapestry of life around us. A skilled bartender's intuition is a dance of observation and empathy, a testament to the profound influence of our environment on our desires."

The classroom ignited with fervent discussions, like a storm of ideas and perspectives clashing, each gust adding depth to the understanding of the paradox. The students marveled at the delicate balance between a bartender's prescience and the customer's autonomy—the beautiful tension between knowing and choosing.

As the orchestrator of this intellectual symphony, I reveled in their enthusiasm, knowing that the Bartender Paradox had stirred a hunger for deeper contemplation within them.

In that classroom, amid the ebb and flow of ideas, the students departed with a new found appreciation for the intricacies of human decision-making—the colorful interplay between external influences and the autonomy of the soul. The Bartender Paradox etched itself indelibly in their minds, a riddle to ponder and cherish, forever guiding them to question the origins of their desires.

As the lesson drew to a close, I knew that my role as a teacher had been fulfilled, leaving my students not only with knowledge but also with the fervor to explore the enigmas that shape our perception of the world. The Bartender Paradox had left an indelible mark on their journey of intellectual discovery, forever guiding them through the labyrinth of life's mysteries.

***

Questions to Ponder

1. How does the Bartender Paradox challenge our belief in free will and autonomy? Does the existence of a bartender who can anticipate our desires before we express them suggest that our choices are predetermined or influenced by external factors?

2. Reflecting on the story, what implications does the Bartender Paradox have for our understanding of personal agency and the power of observation? How does the bartender's ability to anticipate desires through attentive observation challenge our perception of individual autonomy?

3. In what ways does the Bartender Paradox intersect with the concept of determinism? Can the knowledge and understanding of external factors, as demonstrated by the bartender, coexist with our sense of personal freedom and responsibility?

4. Consider the role of empathy in the Bartender Paradox. How does the bartender's deep understanding of their customer's preferences and desires shape

their ability to anticipate choices? Does this suggest that empathy and connection influence our decision-making process?

5. How can we reconcile the Bartender Paradox with our desire for personal autonomy and the belief in our own decision-making abilities? Does the paradox challenge us to reevaluate the nature of choice and consider the complex interplay between internal desires, external influences, and the power of observation?

Chapter 12

EXPECTING THE UNEXPECTED

***

"If you do not expect the unexpected you will not find it, for it is not to be reached by

search or trail."

Heraclitus

***

I stood before my eager students, thrilled to take them on an exhilarating journey into the mind-bending world of paradoxes. Today, I had a special treat for them—the enigmatic and perplexing Unexpected Hanging Paradox. I could already sense the anticipation in the air as they awaited the unveiling of this intellectual puzzle.

"Good day, class!" I greeted them with a twinkle in my eye. "Today, get ready to buckle up your brains as we dive into the captivating universe of the Unexpected Hanging Paradox. Brace yourselves for a wild ride!"

The students leaned forward in their seats; their intrigue sparked by my infectious enthusiasm. "Imagine a prisoner on death row," I began, setting the stage for the unfolding tale. "The judge decides to play a devious game with the prisoner's fate. The condemned person is informed that they will be executed any day between Monday and Friday, but it will come as a surprise—a twist that will keep them on the edge of their seat. They quickly reason they cannot be hanged on Friday because it wouldn't be unexpected. But lo and behold, on a fateful Friday, the hangman pays an unexpected visit, and the prisoner's logical deduction is shattered as they meet their untimely end!"

A wave of awe and bewilderment washed over the room as the students tried to wrap their minds around the paradoxical scenario. I paused, allowing the intrigue to simmer.

"The Unexpected Hanging Paradox," I continued, "throws a wrench into our logical reasoning and challenges our assumptions about certainty. It whispers a tantalizing question: can we ever truly predict the unexpected? Can we ever fully grasp the twists and turns that life might throw?"

One brave soul raised their hand, their eyes searching for clarity amid the paradoxical fog. "But, how do we make sense of this mind-bending enigma? Does it mean our reasoning is flawed, or we can never be sure of anything?"

I grinned, impressed by their keen inquiry. "Ah, my intrepid thinker," I replied, "the Unexpected Hanging Paradox beckons us into the realm of uncertainty and the limitations of our knowledge. It showcases that even our most rock-solid logical deductions can be upended by unforeseen circumstances. It's a humbling reminder that life loves to throw us surprises, and we must embrace the unpredictability with a dash of humility and an open mind."

As the class ended, the students couldn't contain their buzzing excitement. The Unexpected Hanging Paradox had ignited their intellectual curiosity, leaving them hungry for more enigmas and challenges.

I watched them leave, knowing that their journey into paradoxes had just begun. The

Unexpected Hanging Paradox would forever dance in their minds, urging them to embrace life's uncertainties and approach logic with a daring spirit. And as I prepared for the next lesson, I felt a surge of joy, knowing that I had sparked a lifelong thirst for unraveling the mysteries that lie at the heart of paradoxes. With a smile, I eagerly looked forward to the next thrilling chapter in our quest for intellectual wonder.

***

Questions to Ponder

1. How does the Unexpected Hanging Paradox challenge our understanding of logical reasoning and the limits of our assumptions? Does it suggest that even the most well-reasoned deductions can be undermined by unforeseen circumstances?

2. Reflecting on the story, what implications does the Unexpected Hanging Paradox have for our perception of control and predictability in life? Does it invite us to embrace the inherent uncertainty and unpredictability of the future?

3. In what ways does the Unexpected Hanging Paradox intersect with the concept of knowledge and our ability to anticipate the unexpected? Can we genuinely expect events that defy our logical deductions and assumptions?

4. Consider the role of evidence and new information in the context of the Unexpected Hanging Paradox. How does it challenge us to be open-minded and willing to revise our beliefs in the face of unexpected revelations?

5. How can we apply the lessons from the Unexpected Hanging Paradox to our everyday lives? Does it encourage us to approach situations with a sense of humility, recognizing that our assumptions and logical deductions may not always align with the complexities of reality?

Chapter 13

WHAT IS TRULY TRUE?

***

"Face reality as it is ... not as you wish it

to be."

Jack Welch

***

I stood before an eager group of students, ready to take them on an intellectual roller coaster through the mesmerizing realm of paradoxes. Today's destination was the captivating Hooper's Paradox—a mind-bending concept that would push the boundaries of their perception and challenge their grasp on reality.

"Welcome, my dear students!" I greeted them with a glint, thrilled to share this paradoxical journey. "Today, get ready to dive headfirst into the intriguing world of Hooper's Paradox. It's like a mind maze where perception and reality engage in a game of hide-and-seek."

The students leaned in; my mysterious introduction ignited their curiosity. "Picture a brilliant artist named Hooper," I began, setting the stage for the unfolding tale. "His artistry knows no bounds, and he paints a breathtaking landscape so stunningly realistic that it seems to breathe with life. But here's the twist: if the painting is so astonishingly real, how can we be sure that the landscape it depicts isn't just another ingenious stroke of Hooper's brush?"

A hushed silence filled the room as the students grappled with the mind-bending implications. It was as if their imaginations were painting a thousand different possibilities on the canvas of their minds. I let the mystery linger, like a moment frozen in time.

"The Hooper's Paradox shakes the foundation of our perception and challenges us to question what we believe to be true," I continued, my voice tinged with excitement. "It's a playful dance between illusion and reality, urging us to wonder: Can we ever fully trust our senses? What if what we see, hear, or feel is a beautifully crafted mirage?"

A brave student raised their hand, their eyes filled with wonder. "But how do we navigate this labyrinth of perception and reality? Does Hooper's Paradox imply that truth is forever elusive?"

I smiled, proud of their curiosity. "Ah, my astute thinker," I replied, "Hooper's Paradox doesn't seek to undermine our perception or the pursuit of truth. Instead, it's a playful reminder that our unique perspectives and the limitations of our senses color our understanding of reality. It beckons us to approach truth with humility, curiosity, and a willingness to explore the multifaceted nature of reality."

The students left their minds ablaze with curiosity and wonder as the class concluded. The Hooper's Paradox had ignited a spark within them, propelling them on a journey to unravel the complexities of perception and the nature of truth.

I watched them depart, knowing Hooper's Paradox had planted the seeds of exploration and introspection. It would forever linger in their minds, challenging them to question what they perceive and encouraging them to embrace reality's mysterious and beautiful intricacies.

And as I prepared for the next class, I felt excited. The journey through paradoxes had only begun, and I eagerly looked forward to guiding my students through the ever-unfolding mysteries ahead. With a smile, I knew that pursuing truth and the beauty of paradoxes would forever be a fascinating expedition for me and my curious learners.

****

Questions to Ponder

1. How does Hooper's Paradox challenge our perception of reality and the reliability of our senses? Does it suggest that our understanding of truth is subjective and limited by our individual experiences?

2. Reflecting on the story, what implications does Hooper's Paradox have for our pursuit of knowledge and the search for objective truth? Does it suggest that truth may be elusive and that our perceptions can deceive us?

3. In what ways does Hooper's Paradox intersect with the fields of philosophy and epistemology? How does it prompt us to question the nature of reality and the foundations of our knowledge?

4. Consider the role of perspective in the context of Hooper's Paradox. How does our perception shape our understanding of truth? Can we ever truly separate our subjective experiences from the objective reality?

5. How can we apply the insights from Hooper's Paradox to our daily lives? Does it encourage us to approach our interactions and interpretations with humility, recognizing that our biases and limitations influence our understanding of truth?

Chapter 14

FREE WILL

***

"People demand freedom of speech as a
compensation for the freedom of

thought which they

seldom use."

Søren Kierkegaard

***

I found myself facing a classroom buzzing with anticipation. Today, I had the honor of guiding my students through the intricate labyrinth of human existence—the perplexing paradox of free will. It was a topic that had fascinated and confounded thinkers for centuries, and I couldn't wait to dive into its depths with my eager learners.

"Welcome, my dear students," I greeted them with a warm and pensive smile. "Today, we embark on a journey into the enigmatic realm of free will—a concept that dares us to question the essence of choice and agency."

Their eyes locked onto mine, captivated by the weighty subject ahead. I began to weave the threads of the paradox, navigating through the complexity of determinism and the shades of causality that painted the canvas of our lives.

As I shared various philosophical perspectives on free will, I urged my students to challenge their own beliefs and preconceptions. We explored the notion that our decisions might be influenced by many factors—external circumstances and the hidden landscapes of our minds.

Silence enveloped the room as the students grappled with the implications. Was their autonomy just an illusion, or did they possess a genuine ability to shape their destinies? The paradox tugged at the fabric of their understanding like a playful tug-of-war between fate and free will.

With a glimmer of mischief, I posed the questions that perplexed scholars throughout the ages. "Can we truly say we are the architects of our choices, or are we simply the players in a grand cosmic symphony of causality? And if external factors beyond our control influence our decisions, can we still be held morally accountable for our actions?"

The room was filled with spirited debates as the students immersed themselves in the quest for answers. They wrestled with the enigma of free will, peering into the depths of their own souls to discern the dance between choice and circumstance.

As the class drew to a close, I reminded my students that the paradox of free will was a journey without a final destination—a lifelong pursuit of understanding and self-discovery. Their minds buzzed with intellectual curiosity, eager to continue unraveling the complexities of human existence.

As they filed out of the classroom, I couldn't help but feel a surge of satisfaction. My role as a teacher went beyond presenting information— it was about sparking the flames of curiosity and guiding my students on their own philosophical voyages.

The paradox of free will would forever be etched in their minds, propelling them to seek answers, challenge assumptions, and embrace the beautiful intricacies of what it means to be human. And with that, I eagerly awaited the next opportunity to explore the mysteries of the universe with my bright and curious learners.

***

Questions to Ponder

1. How does the paradox of free will challenge our understanding of personal agency and the concept of choice? Does it suggest that our perceived freedom is an illusion, or can we reconcile determinism with our decision-making experience?

2. Reflecting on the story, what implications does the paradox of free will have for moral responsibility and accountability? How can we hold individuals responsible for their actions if external factors and predetermined circumstances influence their choices?

3. In what ways does the paradox of free will intersect with the fields of philosophy and

neuroscience? How can we bridge the gap between philosophical inquiries into free will and scientific studies of human behavior and decision-making?

4. Consider the implications of the paradox of free will for societal structures and legal systems. How can we balance recognizing external influences on individual choices and maintaining a sense of personal responsibility and justice?

5. How can an understanding of the paradox of free will impact our personal lives and relationships? Does it prompt us to approach our interactions with others with empathy and compassion, recognizing that their choices are influenced by a complex interplay of factors beyond their control?

Chapter 15

INFINITE POSSIBILITIES

***

"When you become comfortable with
uncertainty, infinite possibilities

open up in your life."

Eckhart Tolle

***

I stood before a classroom filled with eager
students, ready to journey through the
intriguing realm of numbers and the
captivating Interesting Number Paradox.
Today, I aimed to challenge their perception of
mathematical patterns and infinite possibilities.

"Good morning, class!" I greeted them with a
twinkle in my eye. "Today, we delve into the
fascinating world of numbers and the
Interesting Number Paradox—a puzzle that
challenges our understanding of randomness

and the human desire to seek patterns in the most unexpected places."

The students leaned forward, captivated by the enigmatic subject at hand. I continued, guiding them through the complexities of the paradox. I shared stories of unexpected patterns found in number sequences and the human tendency to search for meaning in randomness.

As I unfolded the mysteries of the Interesting Number Paradox, I encouraged my students to question their assumptions about mathematical patterns and explore the delicate balance between order and chaos. I ignited their curiosity by showcasing examples of seemingly random numbers that revealed surprising ways upon closer inspection.

The room buzzed with excitement as the students marveled at the paradoxical nature of numbers. How could apparent randomness yield hidden order? What implications did this paradox have for our understanding of mathematics and the nature of reality?

As the class drew close, I posed thought-provoking questions to stimulate further exploration. How does the Interesting Number

Paradox challenge our perception of randomness? Can we find beauty and meaning in patterns that emerge from seemingly chaotic sequences?

With their minds ablaze, the students left the classroom, showing a newfound appreciation for the mysterious nature of numbers. They understood that mathematics was not just about solving equations but an adventure of infinite wonder and paradoxical surprises.

Watching them depart, I couldn't help but feel a sense of fulfillment. My role as a teacher was not just about transmitting knowledge but nurturing their curiosity and encouraging them to embrace the magic of mathematics.

The Interesting Number Paradox had left its mark on their hearts and minds, urging them to continue exploring the hidden patterns and enchanting paradoxes within the endless universe of numbers. And so, I looked forward to our next voyage into the wonders of mathematics, where we would continue unraveling the enigmas that make this discipline an unending source of fascination and delight.

Questions to Ponder

1. How does the Interesting Number Paradox challenge our perception of randomness and pattern-seeking? Does it suggest hidden patterns in seemingly chaotic sequences, or is our tendency to find order a mere illusion?

2. Reflecting on the story, what implications does the Interesting Number Paradox have for our understanding of mathematics as a tool for understanding the universe? How does it shape our perception of the inherent beauty and complexity of numbers?

3. Can exploring the Interesting Number Paradox extend beyond mathematics and into other fields of study? How might the paradox influence our understanding of randomness and patterns in science, art, or human behavior?

4. Consider the relationship between creativity and the Interesting Number Paradox. How might embracing the paradoxical nature of numbers inspire new

insights and innovations in various fields?
How can we harness the power of paradox
to spark creative thinking?

5. How does the study of the Interesting
    Number Paradox influence our perspective
    on the concept of certainty? Does it
    challenge our belief in absolute truth and
    certainty, suggesting that uncertainty and
    paradox are fundamental aspects of our
    world?

Chapter 16

WHEEL OF FATE

***

"Be extremely subtle, even to the point of

formlessness. Be extremely mysterious,

even to the point of soundlessness.

Thereby you can be the director

of the opponent's fate."

Sun Tzu

***

I stood before a class of eager students, ready to journey through the intricate concepts of philosophy and the captivating Aristotle's Wheel Paradox. Today, we will explore the mind-bending nature of motion and the enigmatic relationship between perpetual motion and change.

"Greetings, my curious learners," I greeted them with a warm smile, sensing their anticipation for the intellectual adventure that awaited us. "Today, we shall venture into the captivating world of philosophy and the mind-boggling Aristotle's Wheel Paradox—a puzzle that challenges our understanding of motion and its connection to change."

The students leaned forward, their minds brimming with curiosity as they eagerly awaited the unraveling of the paradox. I began to explain the essence of the paradox—a wheel rolling downhill, and yet, Aristotle posited that it would never reach the bottom if its center of mass moved at a constant speed.

As I navigated the complexities of Aristotle's Wheel Paradox, we embarked on a thought experiment together. We delved into the depths of motion, velocity, and the intriguing role of perception in grasping the nature of change. We danced through the realms of time and explored the paradoxical notion that an object could be in constant motion yet never quite reach its final destination.

With each passing moment, the paradox challenged our preconceptions, leaving us in awe of the intricate connections between motion, change, and our perception of reality. We were unraveling a cosmic puzzle, piecing together the enigmatic tapestry of existence.

As the class drew to a close, I encouraged the students to reflect on the philosophical implications of Aristotle's Wheel Paradox. How did this paradox challenge our understanding of motion, change, and the very concept of infinity? Did it suggest the limitations of our human faculties in grasping the fundamental nature of reality?

Inspired by our journey through the paradox, the students left the classroom with their minds buzzing, carrying a newfound appreciation for the complexities of philosophy. They understood that knowledge was not always linear or straightforward but intertwined with paradoxes that invited us to delve deeper and question our assumptions.

As I watched them depart, a sense of fulfillment washed over me, knowing that I had ignited a spark of intellectual curiosity within my students. Aristotle's Wheel Paradox would forever be etched in their minds, urging them to continue questioning, pondering, and embracing the enigmatic nature of existence.

And as I prepared for my next class, I knew that my role as a teacher went beyond imparting facts—it was about nurturing a love for philosophical inquiry and guiding my students to challenge assumptions and seek more profound truths. Aristotle's Wheel Paradox would serve as a guiding star, leading them on a lifelong journey of intellectual wonder and reminding them that pursuing knowledge is a thrilling exploration of paradoxical phenomena.

***

Questions to Ponder

1. How does Aristotle's Wheel Paradox challenge our conventional understanding of motion and change? What insights does it offer into the nature of time and our perception of reality?

2. Reflecting on the story, what philosophical implications does Aristotle's Wheel Paradox have regarding infinity? Does it suggest that certain aspects of reality might be beyond our grasp or understanding?

3. Consider the relationship between perception and truth in the context of Aristotle's Wheel Paradox. How does our perception of motion and change influence our understanding of reality? Can we rely solely on our senses to uncover deeper truths about the world?

4. How does Aristotle's Wheel Paradox intersect with other philosophical concepts, such as Zeno's paradoxes? Do these paradoxes share common threads in challenging our understanding of motion and the nature of existence?

5. In light of Aristotle's Wheel Paradox, what implications does it have for our daily lives and decision-making processes? How might an awareness of paradoxes in philosophy influence our approach to problem-solving and our perceptions of progress?

Chapter 17

THE PATH TO OUR DESTINATION

***

"I can't change the direction of the wind, but I can adjust my sails to always reach my destination."

Jimmy Dean

***

I stood before my class, ready to embark on a captivating journey through the fascinating world of philosophy and the mind-bending Zeno's Paradox. Today was a day of exploration, where I aimed to challenge my student's understanding of motion, infinity, and the very fabric of reality.

"Good day, my curious minds," I greeted my students with a sparkle in my eyes. "Today, we dive into the intriguing realm of philosophy and the thought-provoking Zeno's Paradox—a puzzle that questions the essence of motion and the mind-boggling concept of infinity."

The students leaned forward, their curiosity piqued, as I skillfully unfolded the paradox before them. I described Zeno's mind-boggling series of arguments, each seemingly simple yet profound, challenging the idea of continuous motion and the possibility of ever reaching a destination.

As I guided my students through the paradox, I ignited their imaginations with vivid thought experiments. We pondered the notion of an arrow in flight, perpetually halving its distance to the target yet never quite reaching it. We ventured into the realm of Achilles and the tortoise, exploring the limitations of infinite divisibility.

Together, we grappled with the paradox's profound implications. How could motion exist if there were always infinite intervals to traverse? Did Zeno's Paradox reveal inherent limitations in our understanding of the physical world and the very nature of reality itself?

As the class drew to a close, I encouraged my students to reflect on the broader philosophical questions raised by Zeno's Paradox. How does it challenge our perception of time, space, and the fundamental fabric of the universe? Can we ever truly comprehend the concept of infinity, or is it an enigma that eludes our grasp?

Inspired by our journey into the depths of philosophy, the students left the classroom with their minds buzzing with new insights and questions. They realized that pursuing knowledge was an endless adventure that demanded critical thinking and a willingness to embrace paradoxes.

I observed my students depart, satisfied knowing I had ignited their intellectual curiosity. Zeno's Paradox would forever linger in their minds, urging them to question, explore, and embrace the enigmatic nature of existence.

And as I prepared for my next class, I reflected on the profound role of a teacher—to ignite a thirst for knowledge, challenge assumptions, and guide students on a path of intellectual discovery. Zeno's Paradox would be a constant reminder of the limitless depths of philosophy and the unending quest for understanding.

***

Questions to Ponder

1. How does Zeno's Paradox challenge our conventional understanding of motion and the possibility of reaching a destination? What does it reveal about the nature of time and the concept of infinity?

2. Reflecting on the story, what philosophical implications does Zeno's Paradox have regarding the limitations of human perception and our ability to comprehend the infinitely small and infinitely large?

3. Consider the relationship between mathematics and philosophy in the context of Zeno's Paradox. How does mathematical reasoning help us unravel the paradox and explore the boundaries of motion and infinity?

4. How might Zeno's Paradox intersect with other philosophical concepts, such as the concept of change and the nature of existence? Does it challenge our understanding of reality and the notion of progress?

5. What can Zeno's Paradox teach us about embracing ambiguity and uncertainty in our daily lives? How might an awareness of paradoxes in philosophy influence our decision-making and our perceptions of time, achievement, and personal growth?

Chapter 18

RANDOMNESS

***

"So much of life, it seems to me, is determined by pure randomness."

Sidney Poitier

***

I stood before my students, ready to embark on an intriguing journey into the concept of the Lottery Paradox. With a sparkle in my eyes, I knew this lesson would challenge their understanding of randomness and the mysteries of human intuition.

"Good morning, class!" I greeted them with a warm smile. "Today, we venture into the perplexing realm of the Lottery Paradox, where the nature of chance and our perceptions of probability collide."

The students leaned forward, eager to unravel the mysteries of this enigmatic paradox. I explained the paradox, illustrating how our intuition often clashes with statistical reasoning regarding lottery games.

Through interactive discussions and captivating examples, I guided my students to question their assumptions. Together, we grappled with the paradoxical idea that despite the astronomical odds of winning the lottery, someone always manages to win.

As we explored the implications of the Lottery Paradox, we delved into its deeper meaning. Did this paradox reveal flaws in our understanding of probability? What did it teach us about the human tendency to assign meaning to random events?

As the class concluded, I encouraged my students to reflect on the broader implications of the Lottery Paradox. How did it challenge their perceptions of luck and fortune? What lessons could be learned about risk and reward?

Inspired by our journey into the world of probabilities, the students left the classroom with a renewed appreciation for the complexity of chance. They realized that while luck plays a significant role, it is essential to approach probabilities with a rational mindset and an understanding of statistical principles.

I observed my students depart, knowing I had sparked their curiosity and fostered a deeper understanding of the Lottery Paradox. This newfound insight will help them navigate a world of uncertainties and make more informed decisions based on sound reasoning.

And as I prepared for my next class, I felt a sense of fulfillment, knowing that I had instilled in my students a lifelong appreciation for the delicate balance between chance and reason. The Lottery Paradox would forever resonate in their minds, reminding them to approach probability critically and appreciate the enigmatic nature of randomness.

***

Questions to Ponder

1. How does the Lottery Paradox challenge our intuitive understanding of probability and randomness?

2. What does the paradox teach us about the human tendency to assign meaning to random events, such as winning the lottery?

3. In what ways does the Lottery Paradox highlight the complexities of risk and reward in games of chance?

4. How can a deeper understanding of the paradox help individuals make more informed decisions regarding gambling and other situations involving probabilities?

5. What broader implications does the Lottery Paradox have for our perceptions of luck and fortune, and how might it influence our approach to taking calculated risks in life?

Chapter 19

POWER IN REASON

***

"A man always has two reasons for doing anything: a good reason and the

real reason."

J. P. Morgan

***

I stood before my students, eager to explore the perplexing concept of the Omnipotence Paradox. With a calm and contemplative demeanor, I knew this lesson would challenge my students' understanding of power's nature and logical reasoning's intricacies.

"Good morning, class!" I greeted them with a gentle smile. "Today, we embark on a journey into the fascinating realm of the Omnipotence Paradox, where the very notion of unlimited power leads us down a path of profound philosophical questions."

The students leaned forward, intrigued by the enigma that awaited them. I carefully explained the paradox, illustrating how the idea of an all-powerful being leads to logical contradictions and puzzles that challenge our understanding of possibility.

Through thought-provoking discussions and intricate examples, I guided my students to question their assumptions. Together, we grappled with the paradoxical nature of a being who can do anything, including creating a task they cannot accomplish—an idea that seems to defy the very concept of omnipotence.

As we explored the implications of the Omnipotence Paradox, we delved into its deeper philosophical meaning. Did it challenge the traditional notions of omnipotence and its compatibility with logical consistency? What did it teach us about the limits of power and the paradoxical nature of absolutes?

As the class concluded, I encouraged my students to reflect on the broader implications of the Omnipotence Paradox. How did it shape their understanding of omnipotence, agency, and the nature of existence? What lessons could be learned about the limitations of power and the complexities of logical reasoning?

Inspired by our exploration, the students left the classroom with a new found appreciation for the intricate nature of omnipotence. They realized that power, even in its most absolute form, may encounter logical paradoxes and philosophical dilemmas that challenge our understanding of reality.

I observed my students depart, confident that I had sparked their curiosity and ignited a deeper understanding of the Omnipotence Paradox. This new found insight would encourage them to question assumptions, critically analyze ideas and embrace the complexities of power and logic.

And as I prepared for my next class, I felt a sense of fulfillment, knowing that I had nurtured a group of students who would continue to explore the depths of philosophy and grapple with the paradoxes of existence. The Omnipotence Paradox would forever resonate in their minds, urging them to explore the boundaries of power and reason and to seek wisdom in the face of complexity.

***

Questions to Ponder

1. How does the Omnipotence Paradox challenge our understanding of power and the concept of an all-powerful being?

2. What are the logical contradictions that arise when contemplating the notion of omnipotence?

3. How does the paradoxical nature of omnipotence relate to the broader philosophical questions of free will and determinism?

4. Can the Omnipotence Paradox be reconciled with traditional theological beliefs about a supreme being?

5. What does the paradox teach us about the limitations of power and the complexities of logical reasoning?

Chapter 20

TRUE OR FALSE?

***

"Letters couldn't care less whether what is
written with them is true or false."

Augusto Roa Bastos

***

In a dimly lit classroom, I stood before my
intrigued students. Today's lesson promised to
be fascinating as I introduced them to the mind-
boggling Liar Paradox—a paradox that would
challenge their perception of truth and logic.

"Welcome, my curious minds," I greeted them
with a mischievous smile. "Today, we embark
on a journey into the perplexing world of the
Liar Paradox, a puzzle that will twist your
minds and challenge your understanding of
reality."

The students leaned forward, their eyes wide
with anticipation. I began to paint a vivid
picture of the paradox—a simple statement that

claims it is false. The room filled with confusion and excitement as they grappled with the seemingly contradictory nature of the statement.

With a flair for storytelling, I weaved thought-provoking examples and scenarios into the lesson. We explored ancient tales and modern riddles that teased the fabric of truth and language, leaving the students on the edge of their seats.

As we delved deeper into the Liar Paradox, we questioned the essence of what it means for something to be true or false. Is there a hidden truth to the paradox, or is it a self-referential labyrinth with no escape?

Amid our exploration, I encouraged the students to challenge their assumptions and embrace the chaos of paradoxes. We playfully debated the boundaries of language, wondering if it could ever fully capture the complexities of reality.

As the class drew to a close, the students were left in awe of the enigmatic paradox before them. The Liar Paradox had ignited a fire within them—a burning desire to seek answers to questions that seemed to defy resolution.

As they left the classroom, their minds were abuzz with intellectual curiosity. They knew they were beginning to scratch the surface of the vast world of paradoxes and the mysteries they held.

I watched them depart, my eyes sparkling with satisfaction. I knew that the Liar Paradox had left its mark on their hearts and minds, propelling them on a thrilling journey of philosophical exploration.

And as I prepared for my next class, I couldn't help but smile, knowing that the world of paradoxes had captivated another group of young, curious souls. The Liar Paradox would forever linger in their thoughts, urging them to question, challenge, and embrace the enigmatic nature of truth and logic. For in the realm of paradoxes, the journey of discovery knows no bounds.

***

Questions to Ponder

1. How does the Liar Paradox challenge our understanding of truth and logical consistency?

2. What insights can be gained about the limitations of language and self-reference by exploring the Liar Paradox?

3. How does the Liar Paradox relate to broader philosophical questions about the nature of reality and the reliability of our cognitive systems?

4. Can the Liar Paradox be resolved within existing logical frameworks, or does it expose inherent limitations in our logical systems?

5. What implications does the Liar Paradox have for our everyday communication and the way we navigate the complexities of language and meaning?

Chapter 21

WHEN THE ANSWER IS "NO ANSWER"

***

"The more I think of it, the more I realize there are no answers.

Life is to be lived."

Marilyn Monroe

***

In a bustling classroom, I stood before my students, ready to embark on a thought-provoking journey into the world of paradoxes. Today's topic was the intriguing Barber Paradox, a logical enigma that would challenge their understanding of self-reference and logical consistency.

"Good morning, class!" I greeted them with a smile. "Today, we will explore the captivating Barber Paradox—a puzzle that revolves around a self-referential statement. Are you ready for a mind-bending adventure?"

The students leaned in; their curiosity sparked by the mysterious topic. I carefully explained the paradox, illustrating how the statement "The barber shaves everyone who doesn't shave" creates a logical conundrum when applied to the barber himself.

Through engaging discussions and clever examples, I guided my students to ponder the complexities of the Barber Paradox. They grappled with the idea that he must shave himself if the barber shaves everyone who doesn't shave themselves. But then, wouldn't that mean he should not shave himself as per the statement? It was like chasing one's tail in a circle of contradictions.

Together, we questioned the foundations of logic and the nature of self-reference. How could the paradox challenge our understanding of truth and coherence? What did it reveal about the limitations of language and the intricacies of logical systems?

As the class concluded, I encouraged my students to reflect on the broader implications of the Barber Paradox. How did it relate to questions of meaning, language, and the reliability of logical reasoning? What insights could be gained about the nature of paradoxes and their role in philosophical inquiry?

Inspired by our lively discussion, the students left the classroom with their minds buzzing with intellectual curiosity. They realized that paradoxes were not just abstract puzzles but profound gateways to exploring the depths of human cognition and understanding.

Observing my students depart, I felt satisfied, knowing that I had sparked their interest and challenged their thinking with the Barber Paradox. This philosophical journey would encourage them to question assumptions, explore the intricacies of logic, and embrace the enigmatic nature of paradoxes.

As I prepared for the next class, I felt a thrill of anticipation, eager to introduce my students to more philosophical wonders. The Barber Paradox would forever remain etched in their minds, serving as a reminder that the pursuit of knowledge is a thrilling and never-ending adventure, filled with delightful paradoxes waiting to be explored.

***

Questions to Ponder

1. How does the Barber Paradox challenge our understanding of logic?

2. Is it possible to create a paradox that has no solution?

3. Can paradoxes help us expand our understanding of the world around us?

4. How can we use logic to resolve paradoxes?

5. Can philosophy help us understand and resolve paradoxes that seem unsolvable?

Chapter 22

THOUGHT-PROVOKING DIALOGUE

***

"Don't find fault, find a remedy."

Henry Ford

***

I stood before my philosophy class, eager to unravel the mysteries of paradoxes. Today's topic was the intriguing Drinker Paradox, a concept that had fascinated thinkers for centuries.

"Good morning, class!" I greeted my students with enthusiasm. "Today, we embark on a journey into the enigmatic Drinker Paradox. It revolves around the statement: 'In every non-empty bar, there is someone such that if they are drinking, everyone in the bar is drinking.'"

The students looked intrigued yet puzzled, their minds already working to decipher the paradox. I continued, "At first glance, this statement seems perplexing. How can the drinking behavior of one person affect everyone else in the bar? Can a single individual have such an impact on the entire group?"

I paused, letting the paradox sink in, before leading the class into a lively discussion. We explored different scenarios, considered alternative interpretations, and debated the logical implications of the Drinker Paradox.

As the class progressed, students shared their insights, challenging each other's assumptions and engaging in thought-provoking debates. We contemplated the nature of truth and the complexities of generalizing about groups.

With each question and counterargument, the classroom buzzed with intellectual excitement. The students were fully immersed in the paradox, delving deeper into its complexities and questioning the limits of our understanding.

Finally, as the class drew to a close, I left my students with a final thought, "Is the Drinker Paradox truly a paradox, or can we find a way to resolve the apparent contradiction? Perhaps the answer lies in exploring the subtleties of language and context."

The students left the classroom with their minds racing, eager to explore the Drinker Paradox further. I knew that pursuing understanding paradoxes would fuel their philosophical curiosity and encourage them to embrace the complexities of the human mind.

As I prepared for the next class, I felt fulfilled, knowing I had ignited a spark of intellectual inquiry within my students. The Drinker Paradox would forever linger in their minds, urging them to question, explore, and revel in the enigmatic nature of paradoxes. These tantalizing puzzles continuously challenge our understanding of the world.

***

Questions to Ponder

1. How does the Drinker Paradox challenge our notions of causality and logical reasoning?

2. Can we find a scenario where the statement "If one person is drinking, everyone else is drinking" holds in a non-empty bar?

3. What are the underlying assumptions in the Drinker Paradox, and how do they affect our interpretation of the statement?

4. Does the Drinker Paradox reveal limitations in our ability to make universal claims about groups or situations?

5. How can we apply the principles of logic and critical thinking to navigate paradoxes like the Drinker Paradox and arrive at a deeper understanding of their implications?

Chapter 23

PONDERING THE PAST

***

"The present is what slips by us while we're pondering the past and worrying

about the future."

Ziggy Marley

***

I stood at the front of the lecture hall, ready to delve into the mesmerizing world of time paradoxes. Today's topic was the notorious Grandfather Paradox, a mind-bending idea that had captured the imagination of many.

"Good morning, class!" I greeted the students with a smile. "Today, we embark on a journey into the intricate world of time travel and the Grandfather Paradox."

The students leaned forward in their seats, eager to explore the mysteries of time travel and its paradoxes. I continued, "Imagine this: What would happen if you were to travel back in time and encounter your own grandfather before he has a chance to have children? Would you cease to exist, or could some strange twist of fate unfold?"

The room fell into contemplative silence as the students grappled with the mind-bending implications of the Grandfather Paradox. I guided them through a series of thought experiments, encouraging them to explore possibilities and engage in lively discussions.

Together, we delved into the intricacies of causality and the butterfly effect—how seemingly small actions in the past could have profound consequences in the future. We questioned the idea of free will and whether we could alter the past without creating logical contradictions.

As the class drew to a close, I left my students with a final question: "Does the Grandfather Paradox suggest that time travel is inherently impossible, or are there alternative explanations or resolutions? Could our understanding of time and causality be limited, and there are yet undiscovered secrets of the universe?"

The students left the lecture hall with their minds ablaze, their imaginations ignited by the possibilities of time travel and the mysteries of the Grandfather Paradox. I knew this paradox would continue to haunt their thoughts, urging them to explore the uncharted territories of temporal anomalies and the enigmatic nature of time.

As I prepared for the next lecture, I felt satisfied, knowing I had instilled a sense of wonder and curiosity in my students. The Grandfather Paradox would forever linger in their minds, challenging their perceptions of reality and encouraging them to unravel the secrets of the universe—one paradox at a time.

***

Questions to Ponder

1. What are the different possibilities that arise from the Grandfather Paradox? Can it be resolved coherently and logically?

2. Does the Grandfather Paradox imply that time travel is impossible, or are there other

theories and explanations that can reconcile the paradox?

3. How does the Grandfather Paradox challenge our understanding of causality and the concept of a linear timeline?

4. Can we find alternative ways to understand time travel that avoid the paradox, such as the multiverse theory or the idea of parallel timeline?

5. What are the philosophical and ethical implications of the Grandfather Paradox? How does it impact our notions of free will and the consequences of our actions?